This Toronto

City Guide & Journal

BELONGS TO

....

For Evelyn and Tyler - my little city explorers.

1st Edition
Published November 2022
Copyright © 2022 Aileen Choi.
Published by my little city explorer.

Additional Resources
Visit www.mylittlecityexplorer.com (QR code below) for updated links to attraction websites, restaurant recommendations, and more.

Image Credits
Key: T = top; M = middle; B = bottom; L = left; R = right
Special thanks to all the attractions that provided images and logos.

42ML **Clifton Hills**; 24 **Hockey Hall of Fame**; 40TR, 40BL **LEGOLAND Discovery Centre**; 26 **Little Canada**; 34 **Ontario Science Centre**; 20 **Ripley's Aquarium of Canada**; 32 **ROM**; 36 **Toronto Zoo**; 5, 10TL, 10TR, 22MR, 22BR, 23TR, 29, 30R, 38, 39, 40ML, 40MR, 42BL, 42BR **Aileen Choi**. All other images and design elements **Canva**.

Hi Friends!

This kid's city guide & journal was made just for YOU! Find out all about the FUN things there are to do in the city you are visiting! After learning all about TORONTO, you can share with your grown-ups what interesting places you want to explore. You can also use this book to journal about your adventures exploring the city.

In this book you will find these sections:

HAVE FUN EXPLORING!

my little city explorer
go on adventures   make memories

About Toronto

1 Where in the world is Toronto?

Toronto is the capital city of Ontario. Ontario is a province in Canada. Canada is a country in North America.

DID YOU KNOW? Toronto isn't as northern as you may think! The city is actually further south than cities like Seattle, Washington, USA and Vancouver, British Columbia, Canada. Toronto has the same latitude as Florence, Italy: 43° N.

2 How did Toronto get its name?

The word Toronto comes from the Mohawk word tkaronto, which means "the place in the water where the trees are standing." It was first used to refer to an area near present-day Orillia (around Lake Simcoe and Lake Couchiching). Over time, the name went through various spelling changes: Tarento, Tarontha, Taronto, Toranto, Torento, and Toronton. The City of Toronto was formed on March 6th, 1834.

3 What nicknames does Toronto have?

Toronto has many nicknames, like: T.O., T-Dot, Hogtown, YYZ, and, most recently, The 6ix (pronounced "the six"). Drake (the Canadian rapper) nicknamed Toronto "The 6ix" because the city's first area code was 416. Toronto is also made up of six former areas: Old Toronto, Scarborough, East York, North York, Etobicoke, and York.

Toronto's Motto

Diversity Our Strength

4. What is Toronto known for?

Toronto is known for its many skyscrapers and for being one of the most multicultural cities in the world. People come from all over the world to live in Toronto. There are many ethnic neighbourhoods in Toronto including Chinatown, Greektown, Little Italy, Little India, Koreatown, and more.

5. What currency is used in Toronto?

In Canada, currency comes in the form of bills and coins. The smallest bill is the $5 (five dollars) and the largest is $100. The $1 coin is called the Loonie and the $2 coin is the Toonie. The other coins are the quarter (0.25 or 25 cents), the dime (0.10), and the nickel (0.05).

DID YOU KNOW? Canadian bills are made from thin, flexible plastic known as a polymer. This means they are waterproof!

People of Toronto

1 What do you call people of Toronto?

Torontonians.

2 How do people get around?

Torontonians have many ways of getting around the city. There are buses, a subway system, taxis, and even street cars. A lot of people also get around by walking or biking. There are many bike lanes in the city.

3 What language(s) do Torontonians speak?

The official languages of Canada are English and French. Most Torontonians speak English.

4 How many Torontonians are there?

As of 2022, Toronto is home to more than 2.7 million people, it's the city with the largest population in Canada and the fourth most populated city in North America (after Mexico City, New York City, and Los Angeles). Toronto is often referred to as part of the GTA which stands for the Greater Toronto Area. There are more than 6 million people living in the GTA (which also includes Durham, Halton, Peel, and York Regions).

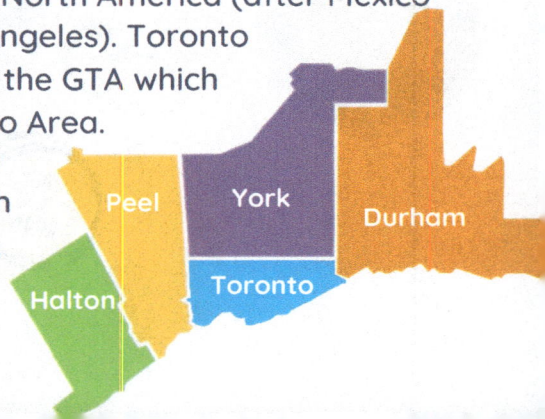

Peel
York
Durham
Toronto
Halton

Toronto Word Search

Words might be forwards, backwards or diagonal!

```
D  P  A  R  K  S  R  G  E  I  N  O  O  T  X
Y  T  I  S  R  E  V  I  D  C  E  O  U  H  V
S  K  Y  S  C  R  A  P  E  R  S  R  R  I  F
A  I  K  D  M  E  R  U  T  N  E  V  D  A  O
M  U  I  I  C  E  S  O  A  T  G  T  N  H  I
A  V  Y  I  I  N  R  E  Y  G  O  O  J  E  R
P  Z  D  N  Y  O  B  W  F  R  H  U  Y  T  A
L  M  O  M  N  M  U  S  E  U  M  S  D  I  T
E  O  A  T  E  W  O  F  G  V  B  U  N  N  N
L  D  O  A  T  T  R  A  C  T  I  O  N  S  O
E  U  E  U  K  P  D  V  P  A  D  A  N  A  C
A  I  J  R  P  N  I  P  Y  T  I  C  L  J  E
F  E  R  O  L  P  X  E  A  I  E  N  P  U  U
```

ADVENTURE	EXPLORE	ONTARIO
ATTRACTIONS	GTA	PARKS
CANADA	LOONIE	SKYSCRAPERS
CITY	MAPLE LEAF	TOONIE
DIVERSITY	MUSEUMS	TORONTO

Answers on page 78

Spring

Take in the wonderful smell of flowers at one of the city's many parks or gardens like Edwards Gardens. For about two weeks in April, see beautiful cherry blossoms throughout the city at places like High Park.

JOKE What do you call a baker's garden?

Summer

Toronto can get very hot in the summer! Explore the outdoors by visiting a beach or picnicking at one of the many parks. There are always many fun outdoor festivals happening. Canada's largest annual fair, CNE or "The Ex", takes place at the end of August during the weeks leading up to Labour Day (first Monday in September). There are plenty of rides, shows and fun weird foods to try. One year there was cotton candy taco and another year there was a s'mores fried chicken sandwich!

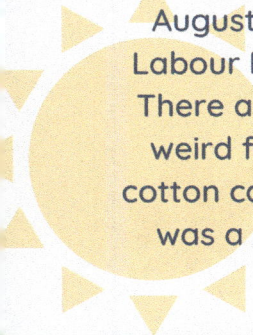

Fall

Toronto has over 10 million trees across the city with plenty of places to see the beautiful orange, yellow, red, purple and brown leaf colours. If you visit Toronto around Halloween, you will find lots of Halloween festivities throughout the city. On October 31st, go door-to-door wearing your Halloween costume and yell "Trick-or-Treat" to get yummy treats!

Fun Every Season

Winter

Remember to bundle up in the winter as it can get very cold. In Toronto, you can enjoy many exciting winter activities such as skiing, snowboarding and tobogganing. Go skating at an outdoor rink like at Nathan Phillips Square. Around Christmas time, you might find Santa and his elves at one of the many malls in the GTA. They could also be at the The Distillery District where there's also lots of festive lights, decorations, and a very tall Christmas tree!

Answer: a flour garden

Foods of Toronto

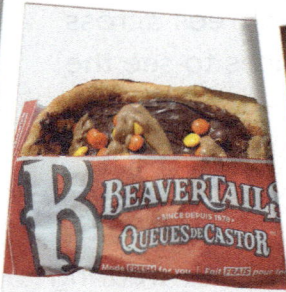

BeaverTails®

These are fried dough pastries, hand stretched to look like a beaver's tail. It's covered with different toppings. Find these at a BeaverTails location.

Poutine

A classic poutine is made of French fries and cheese curds topped with a brown gravy. You can also find other variations throughout the city.

Timbits®

These are round, bite-sized donuts from Tim Hortons (aka Timmies). There are lots of different flavours to choose from like honey dip, chocolate glazed, etc.

Maple Syrup

This is syrup that is made from sap that is collected from Maple trees. It's delicious on top of waffles, pancakes, French toast, and more!

Peameal Bacon

Also known as Canadian bacon, peameal bacon is a perfect breakfast food.

Butter Tarts

A sweet tart made of butter, sugar, syrup, and egg. It's baked in a pastry shell until the filling is semi-solid with a crunchy top.

Count the Snacks.

Count each of the snacks to find out how many there are of each one.

Answers on page 78

11

Places To Explore

Make Your Own Bookmark

Colour and cut out your own bookmark.
Use these bookmarks to mark the places that
you want to visit.

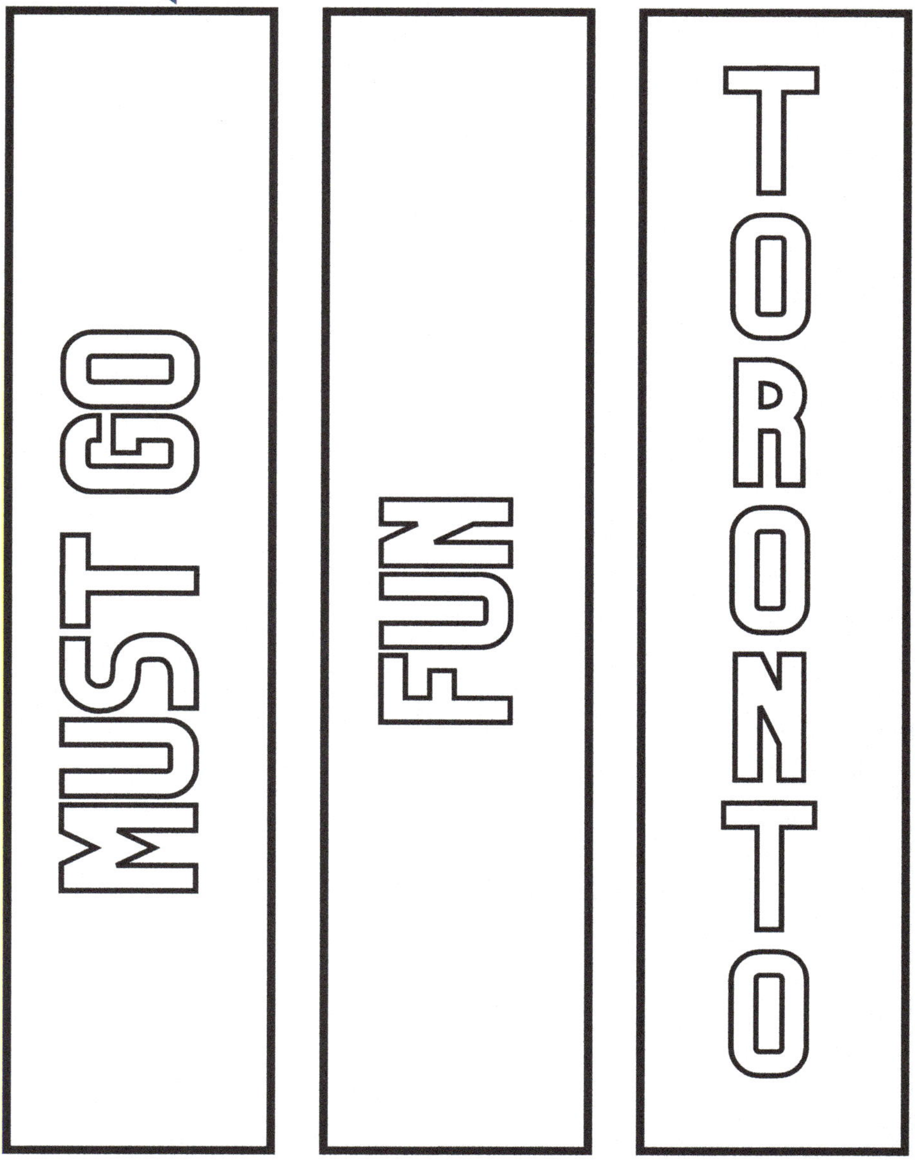

MUST GO

FUN

TORONTO

Don't forget to decorate the back too!

Colour These Toronto Related Items

EXPLORE T.O.

Map of Toronto

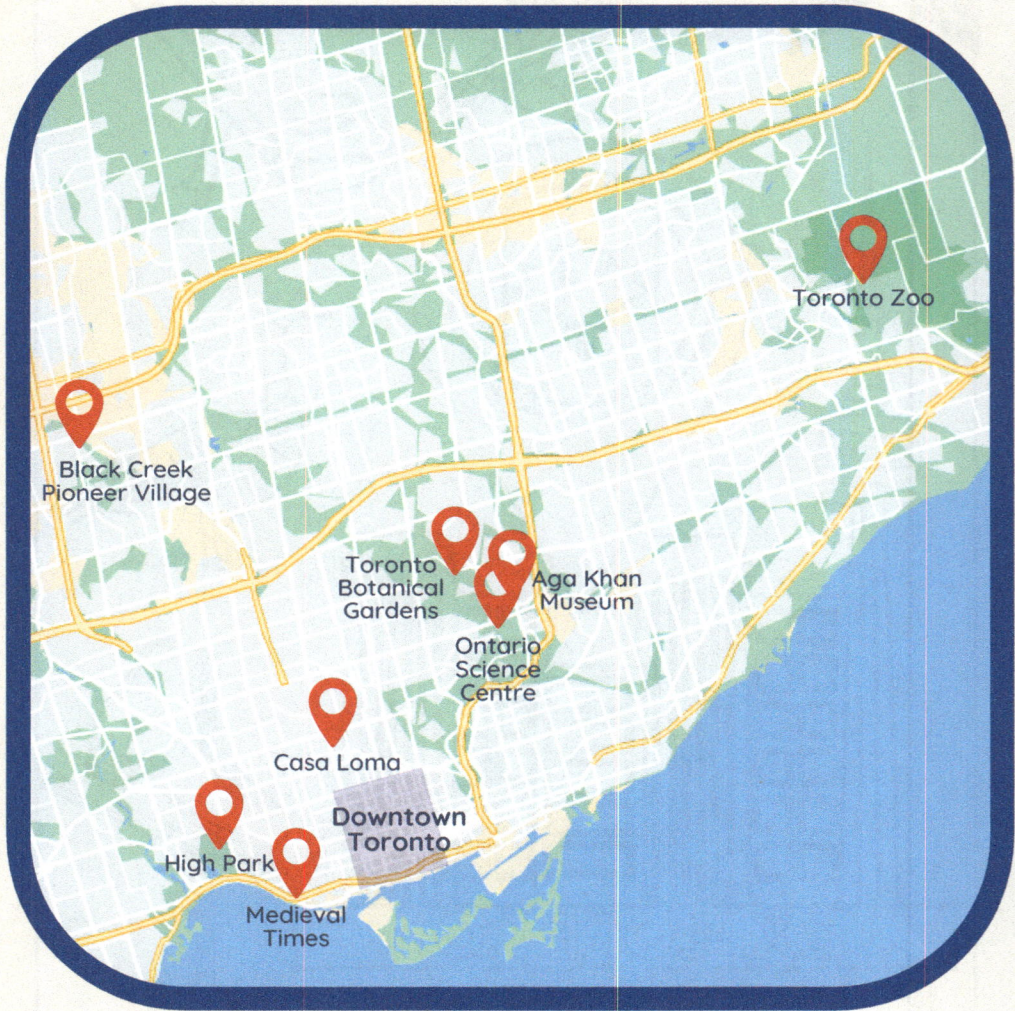

Toronto Zoo

Black Creek
Pioneer Village

Toronto
Botanical
Gardens

Aga Khan
Museum

Ontario
Science
Centre

Casa Loma

Downtown
Toronto

High Park

Medieval
Times

DID YOU KNOW? When there is no traffic it takes about 40 minutes to drive from downtown Toronto to the Toronto Zoo or to Black Creek Pioneer Village.

Map of Downtown Toronto

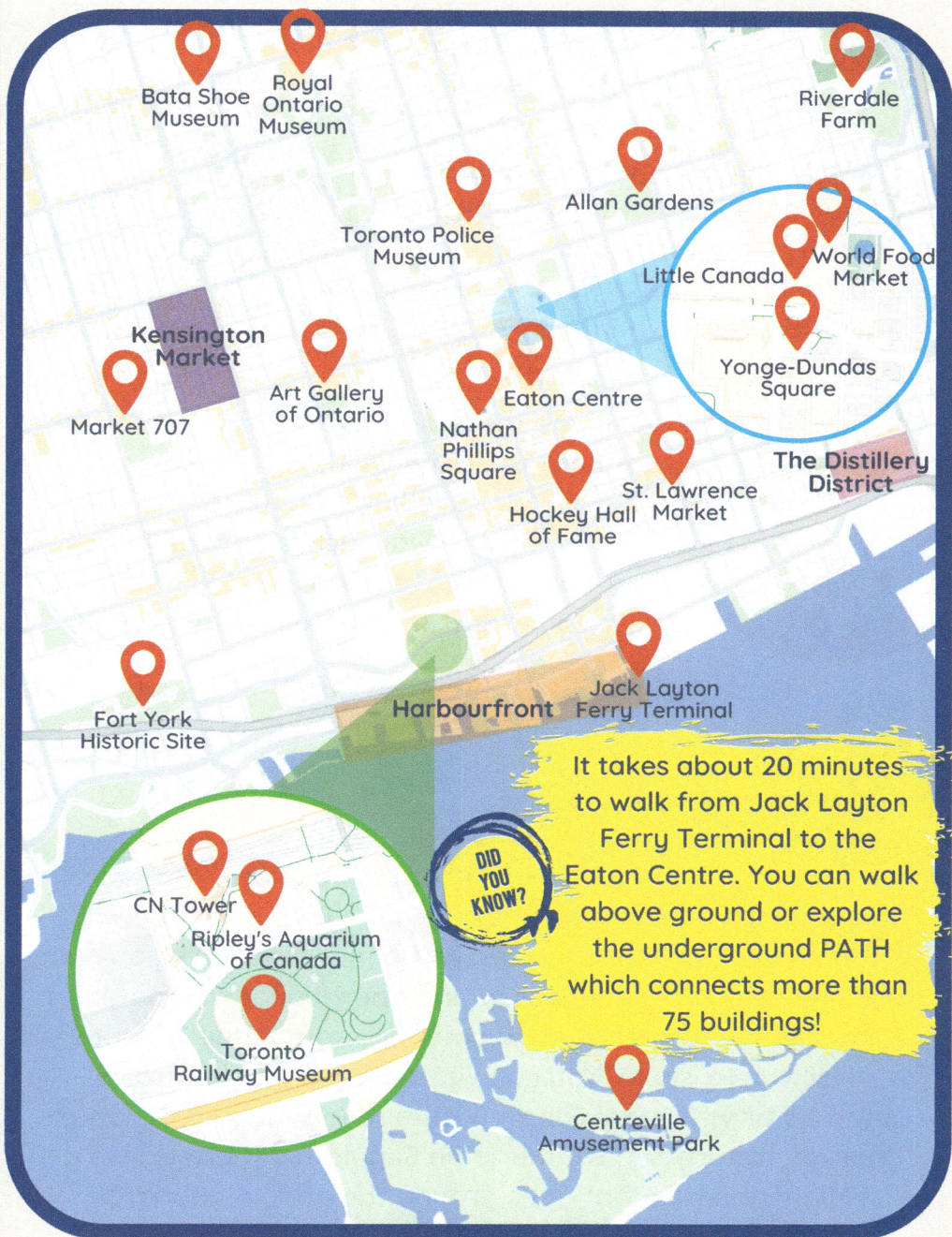

Bata Shoe Museum

Royal Ontario Museum

Riverdale Farm

Allan Gardens

Toronto Police Museum

Little Canada

World Food Market

Kensington Market

Art Gallery of Ontario

Eaton Centre

Yonge-Dundas Square

Market 707

Nathan Phillips Square

The Distillery District

Hockey Hall of Fame

St. Lawrence Market

Fort York Historic Site

Jack Layton Ferry Terminal

Harbourfront

DID YOU KNOW?

It takes about 20 minutes to walk from Jack Layton Ferry Terminal to the Eaton Centre. You can walk above ground or explore the underground PATH which connects more than 75 buildings!

CN Tower

Ripley's Aquarium of Canada

Toronto Railway Museum

Centreville Amusement Park

CN Tower

290 Bremner Boulevard, Toronto

Since 1975, the CN Tower has been a key structure of Toronto's skyline. At 553.33 metres (1815.39 feet) tall, it held the record for the world's tallest freestanding structure up until 2007. To go up the CN Tower, you take a 58 second elevator ride at a speed of 22km/hour (14 miles/hour). That's a lot faster than climbing the 1,776 steps.

All along the Main Observation Level there are floor to ceiling windows. You can see as far as 160km (100 miles)!
Don't forget to walk across, dance along, or cartwheel over the Glass Floor! Look straight down 114 storeys to the ground.

Toronto Railway Museum & Roundhouse Park

255 Bremner Boulevard, Toronto

If you look across the street from the CN Tower you will probably notice a lot of trains. At Roundhouse Park you can see the original, fully restored and operational 120-foot long locomotive turntable. Here you will also find the Toronto Railway Museum. You can wander amongst the trains outdoors or visit the indoor museum to learn about Toronto's railway history and try the Train Simulator. There is also a Mini Train ride that goes around the park. All aboard!

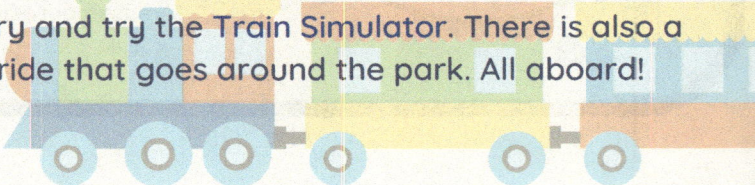

How Many Can You Spot?

Choose a day while you are out exploring to keep track of how many of these you see. Fill in a box each time you see the item!

10						
9						
8						
7						
6						
5						
4						
3						
2						
1						

Ripley's AQUARIUM OF CANADA

288 Bremner Boulevard, Toronto

The aquarium has more than 20,000 sea creatures. You can see aquatic animals like: sharks, jellyfish, unicorn surgeonfish, piranhas, seahorses, clownfish, octopus, and many more!

At the Dangerous Lagoon, there is an underwater viewing tunnel with the longest moving sidewalk in North America. See sharks, sea turtles, eels, different types of fishes, and others super up close!

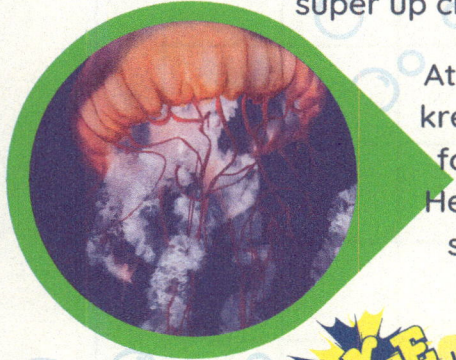

At Planet Jellies, visit one of the largest kreisel tanks (a circular tank that allows for a circular water flow) in the world. Here you will find all kinds of jellies like: sea nettle jellies, upside down jellies, moon jellies, etc.

JOKE What fish is best with peanut butter?

You can touch different sea creatures at the aquarium like horseshoe crabs, sharks, and stingrays. Remember to be gentle!

Answer: a jellyfish

Use Your Imagination

Can you imagine a new type of sea creature?
It could be a creature with the head of a shark
and ten tentacles or a fish with wings...
Draw and colour it here! Does it have a name?

Harbourfront

Toronto Neighbourhood

There's always lots of fun activities happening in the area along Lake Ontario between Bathurst & Yonge Streets.

Take a stroll along Lake Ontario. Look across the lake and see if you can spot a plane taking off from Billy Bishop Toronto City Airport.

Get out onto the water on board the Tall Ship Kajama, a traditional 165 foot, three masted Schooner boat cruise. Go on an adventure and travel the high seas with the crew on Pirate Life.

Visit Harbourfront Centre (235 Queens Quay West, Toronto) where there are food and art festivals taking place all summer long.

Walk, climb, or skip along the topsy-turvy WaveDecks that can be found along Queens Quay.

Head over to the Toronto Islands by catching a ferry from Jack Layton Ferry Terminal. The ferries go to Ward's Island, Centre Island, or Hanlan's Point. If you prefer a rockier ride on a smaller boat, take one of the water taxis.

Toronto Island Park

The Toronto Islands are made up of 15 islands that are connected by bridges. It's about a one hour walk from the east end (Ward's Island) to the west end (Hanlan's Point).

Across Toronto Island Park there are many spots to see the Toronto skyline.

Among the islands there are beaches, splash pads, and playgrounds. You can bring your own bike over to the islands or rent a single bike, a tandem bike, or a quadricycle.

See if you can find the Gibraltar Point Lighthouse on Hanlan's Point.

Centre Island

Visit Centreville Amusement Park to find many fun rides like sky ride, bumper boats, flume log ride, and more.

Beside Centreville is Far Enough Farm, a petting zoo with over 40 animals. Other fun areas to explore on Centre Island include Franklin Children's Garden (inspired by Franklin the Turtle stories) & William Meany Maze. Don't get lost!

30 Yonge Street, Toronto

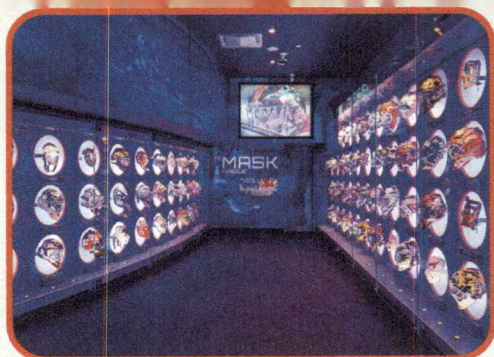

Here you can learn all about the history of ice hockey while exploring lots of fun games. There are many exhibits to visit including Esso Great Hall which is home to the Stanley Cup!

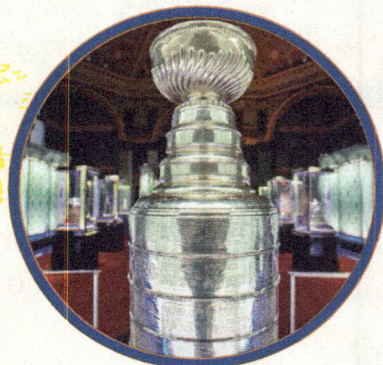

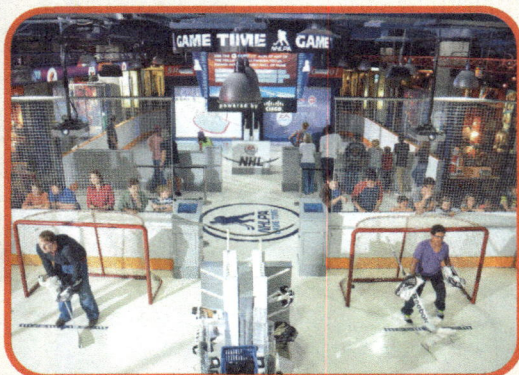

Visit NHLPA Game Time to try the interactive games where you can become a shooter or a goalie against life-size animated hockey superstars.

Take a seat in the TSN Theatre to watch Stanley's Game Seven in 3D or test your sports anchor skills by taking a seat in front of the camera/teleprompter at TSN SportsCentre Studio.

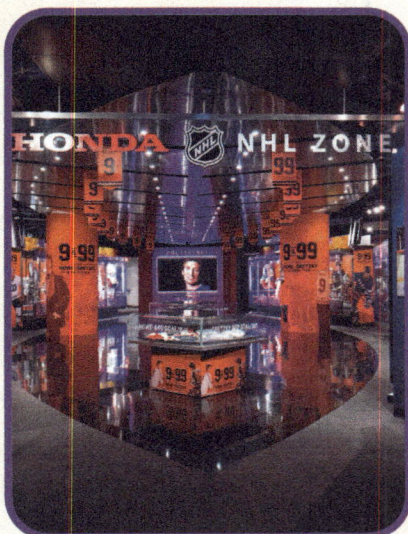

fun & games

Match the Toronto Sports Team

Toronto Raptors **1**

a MLB - Baseball

Toronto Maple Leafs **2**

b NHL - Hockey

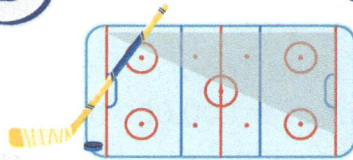

Toronto Blue Jays **3**

c MLS - Soccer

Toronto FC **4**

d CFL - Football

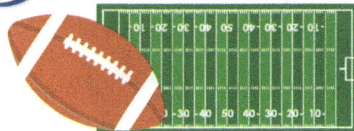

Toronto Argonauts **5**

e NBA - Basketball

Answers on page 78

LITTLE CANADA

OUR HOME AND MINIATURE LAND

10 Dundas Street East Basement 2, Toronto

Here you can see Canada from a different perspective! Take a stroll through Little Canada and see miniature versions of key landmarks and regions. All destinations cycle through day and night time. Be sure to look out for the fireworks at Parliament Hill in Little Ottawa!

 **DID YOU KNOW?** Little Canada was inspired by the Miniatur Wunderland in Hamburg, Germany.

The Build Team at Little Canada have spent over 200,000 hours building out these destinations: Little Toronto, Little Niagara, Little Golden Horseshoe, Little Ottawa, and Petit Québec. The rest of Canada still to come!

You can become little! Go into the Littilization Station to get scanned and 3D printed. You can purchase your own Little Me to take home and/or become a Little Canadian by being placed into miniature Canada.

3/4"
Little Me

Colour the Toronto Flag

Count the coins to figure out which colours to use to colour in the Toronto flag.

$1.05 = Red $1.25 = Blue $2.50 = Purple
$1.10 = Green $2.05 = Orange $3.00 = White

Answers on page 78

Nathan Phillips Square

100 Queen Street West, Toronto

Canada's largest city square is located right in front of Toronto City Hall. Climb on and take photos with the 3D Toronto sign!

DID YOU KNOW? Each letter of the sign weighs about 136kg (300lbs) and can be moved and placed on its own.

Yonge-Dundas Square & Eaton Centre

220 Yonge Street, Toronto

Eaton Centre is the second largest mall in Canada. It's the busiest shopping mall in North America with over 50 million visitors every year. Outside, at the intersection of Yonge and Dundas Streets, you can cross one of the city's busiest pedestrian scramble. Traffic lights in all directions turn red so that people can cross in any direction - even diagonally!

Scavenger Hunt

As you wander through the different alleys in this area, can you spot all of these?

The Distillery District

55 Mill Street, Toronto

LOVE Locks Wall

Soma Chocolatemaker

Little Green Door

Pedestrian Entrance

Big Heart Sculpture

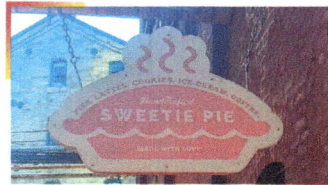
Sweetie Pie

St. Lawrence Market

93 Front Street East, Toronto

Visit one of the world's greatest food markets. With three buildings containing over 120 specialty vendors - there's lots of delicious foods to try!

DID YOU KNOW? Peameal bacon is mainly found in Ontario! Try it at the Carousel Bakery.

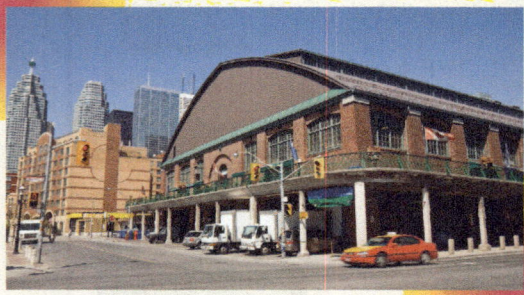

Kensington Market

Toronto Neighbourhood

A neighbourhood area between Bathurst, Spadina, College and Dundas Street West. There's a variety of shops in this area. Explore the different items at Blue Banana Market or try a Korean hot dog at Chung Chun or the Ontario sour cherry pie from Wanda's Pie in the Sky.

Market 707

28 Bathurst Street, Toronto

Here you will find an outdoor shipping container market with unique street food. Grab a poutine from Nom Nom Nom Poutine, a Zimbabwean meat pie from MnandiPies, or some Japanese fried chicken from Gushi.

World Food Market

335 Yonge Street, Toronto

There are more than 15 different food spots to try at this market that is located just up the street from Yonge-Dundas Square. Try churros from Choco Churros or get pastéis from Samba Brazil Eatery.

Name that Food

Toronto has lots of foods from all over the world! How many have you tried?

word bank	phở	churro	soufflé pancake
	takoyaki	beignet	bungeoppang
	dim sum	taco	gulab jamun

a

b

c

d

e

f

g

h

i

Answers on page 79

ROM

100 Queens Park, Toronto

Have you ever wondered how our planet came to life?

Explore the fossils in the Willner Madge Gallery, Dawn of Life to find out and to see one of the oldest rocks on Earth!

Enter The Bat Cave and see over 800 bat models! There's a simulation of the bats in flight during a nightly hunt for food.

DID YOU KNOW?

Bats see with both their eyes and ears! Bats use echolocation (releasing high frequency sound waves and listening to the echo) to navigate.

The Royal Ontario Museum (ROM) is Canada's largest and busiest museum of world cultures, art, and natural history.

Want to touch mossy frogs, a shark jaw, or a snake skin? You can at the Patrick and Barbara Keenan Family Gallery of Hands-on Biodiversity.

See the largest real dinosaur skeleton (Gordo) in Canada. At 27m long (that's like two school buses), Gordo is one of only three complete Barosaurus skeletons on display in the world!

Name that Dinosaur

B _____

1

2

V _____

3

T _____

4

S _____

5

A _____

6 T _____

Answers on page 79

ONTARIO SCIENCE CENTRE

770 Don Mills Road, Toronto

There are many exhibits to explore at the Ontario Science Centre like The Living Earth where you can visit a rain forest, crawl through a cave, and see real poison dart frogs, lizards, turtles, and more!

One of the first interactive science museums in the world, and a place where you can have fun and discover ways to think like a scientist!

Check out the Science Arcade where you can test levers and pulleys, experience a shadow tunnel, and touch a plasma ball.

See your hair stand on end at the static electricity demonstration at the Van de Graaff Generator.

DID YOU KNOW? Ontario Science Centre is built on a ravine, so the floor numbers increase as you go downwards!

Make sure to go to KidSpark, an area made just for kids 8 and under. Here you can pretend to shop in a market, build a roller coaster, farm your own vegetables, play with water, rock out in a music studio, and more!

American Sign Language (ASL)

Use the ASL alphabet chart to figure out the message. What else can you spell?
Try spelling your name!

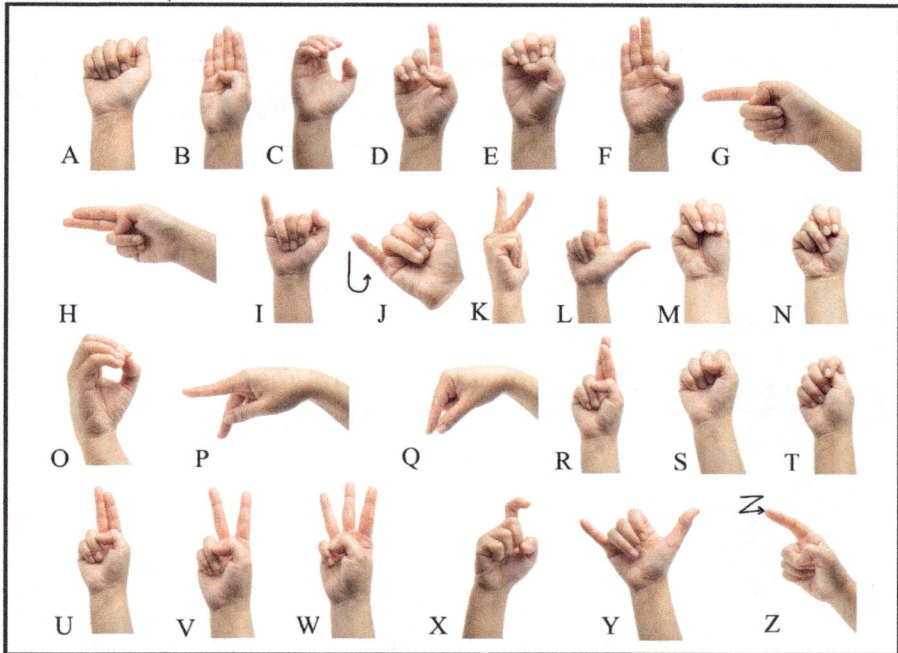

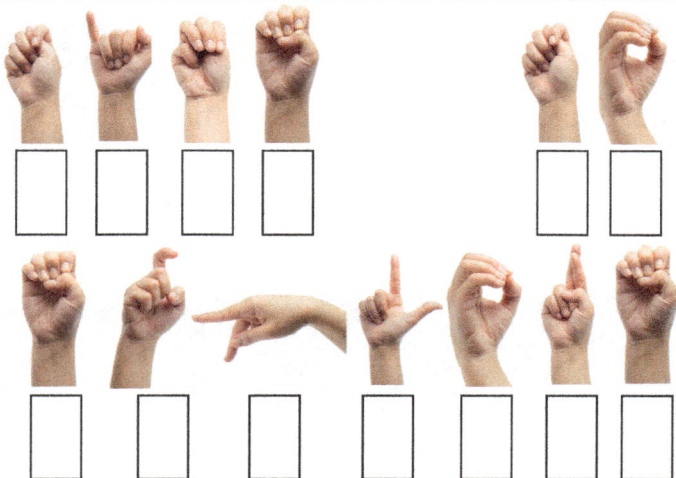

Answers on page 79

toronto ZOO

2000 Meadowvale Road, Toronto

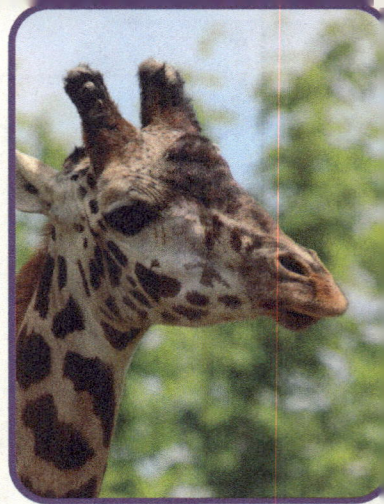

Canada's largest zoo with more than 4000 animals!

Here you can find animals from all over the world such as: African lion, Masai giraffe, ring-tailed lemur, red panda, Sumatran tiger, polar bear, snow leopard, grizzly bear, Komodo dragon, and many, many more!

At the Toronto Zoo, animals and plants are grouped based on where they would naturally be found in the world: Africa, Americas, Australasia, Canadian Domain, Eurasia Wilds, Indo-Malaya, and Tundra Trek.

JOKE What's the funniest nickname to give a tiger?

The Toronto Zoo also has lots of other fun activities including the Zoomobile, the Conservation Carousel, a Kid's Zoo, Splash Island, and more!

Answer: Spots

Use Your Imagination

If you had a zoo, what would your zoo look like?
What animals would be in your zoo?
Draw and colour your zoo below!

Parks & Gardens

High Park

Toronto's largest public park with walking trails, gardens, a wading pool, a swimming pool, and more.

One of the largest outdoor playgrounds in Ontario, the Jamie Bell Adventure Playground is a very special playground because children contributed to the design. In the park there's also a free mini-zoo with animals like: llamas, goats, bison, deer, and peafowls.

DID YOU KNOW? Peafowl is the general name for the family of birds. Peacock is a male and peahen is the female.

Allan Gardens

An indoor botanical garden with six greenhouses.

Toronto Music Garden

An enchanting park inspired by Bach's First Suite for Unaccompanied Cello.

Toronto Botanical Garden & Edwards Garden

Find 17 themed gardens like the Beryl Ivey Knot Garden and the Carpet Beds that hold 15,000 plants.

Beaches

Bluffer's
Centre Island
Cherry/Clarke
Gibraltar Point
Hanlan's Point
Kew-Balmy
Marie Curtis Park East
Rouge
Sunnyside
Ward's Island
Woodbine

On a hot summer day, you can visit one of the 11 Toronto Beaches located along Lake Ontario. Many of the beaches have lifeguards on duty during the summer. The quality of the water is monitored by the city and the city website can be checked to make sure the water is safe to swim. Try building the perfect sand castle on the sandy beaches!

Museums

Aga Khan Museum
A museum dedicated to Islamic art and objects.

Toronto Police Museum & Discovery Centre
Learn about the past and present of policing in Toronto.

Bata Shoe Museum
The world's largest collection of shoes and footwear related items.

History

Fort York Historic Site
Learn about Fort York's history and immerse yourself in the Battle of York.

Black Creek Pioneer Village
Explore how people lived a hundred years ago.

Casa Loma
Explore the castle's secret passages and tunnels.

Other Places

Riverdale Farm
A working farm in the middle of a park! Here you can visit farm animals like: cows, pigs, sheep, goats, and chickens.

Art Gallery of Ontario
Over 90,000 works of art can be found at the AGO.

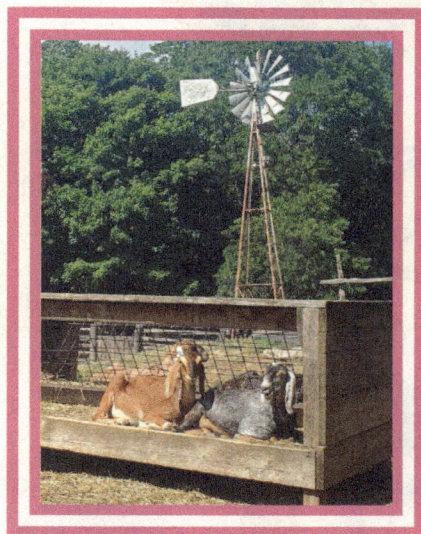

Medieval Times Dinner & Tournament
Enjoy a feast and cheer on your knight in a tournament.

LEGOLAND®
DISCOVERY CENTRE

1 Bass Pro Mills Drive, Vaughan

The only LEGOLAND® Discovery Centre in Canada is located inside Vaughan Mills, an indoor outlet mall with over 200 stores and restaurants. Here you will find lots of LEGO® bricks to build with. Create your own racecar and race it down the speed ramp!

Go on the LEGO themed rides Merlin's Apprentice and Kingdom Quest. Watch one (or all four) of the movies featuring LEGO characters in the LEGO 4D Cinema. Put on the special glasses and don't be surprised if you feel wind, rain, or maybe even snow!

DID YOU KNOW?

The Guinness World Records for the largest LEGO brick flag was built at this LEGOLAND Discovery Centre. 248,062 bricks were used!

Visit the LEGO replica of the GTA and surrounding area in MINILAND®. See if you can spot the Toronto landmarks like the CN Tower, ROM, Toronto Zoo, and more. MINILAND is made up of nearly 1.5 million LEGO bricks!

Canada's
Wonderland   Reptilia Vaughan
LEGOLAND
Discovery Centre
Toronto

Just north of Toronto, in Vaughan (located in York Region), there are some more fun attractions to visit.

Toronto

DID YOU KNOW? When there is no traffic it takes about 40 minutes to drive from downtown Toronto to these attractions.

Reptilia Zoo
2501 Rutherford Road, Vaughan

Canada's largest indoor reptile zoo
with over 250 animals like snakes,
turtles, crocodiles, and more.
Go meet the reptiles, stay for a show,
and see a feeding session.

Canada's Wonderland
1 Canada's Wonderland Drive, Vaughan

Canada's first and largest
amusement park! Spend a whole
day here going on the rides, visiting
the water park, watching shows,
and playing the many games.
Don't forget to try the delicious
funnel cake!

Niagara Falls

Niagara Falls is a great city to visit with one of the most amazing waterfalls in the world. It is only a 1.5 hour drive from Toronto!

There are many fun attractions to explore in Niagara Falls including the Voyage to the Falls Boat Tour where you get on a boat that takes you right near the falls. You get a poncho to wear, but you will still get wet! To get another view of the falls, go to Journey Behind the Falls. If you enjoy heights, go on the Whirlpool Aero Car, or you can test your climbing skills at WildPlay Whirlpool Adventure Course.

Three waterfalls make up the Niagara Falls: the American Falls, the Bridal Veil Falls, and the largest, the Horseshoe Falls!

Take time to explore Clifton Hill, known as the "Street of Fun". Here you will find attractions like: wax museums, haunted houses, mini-golf, go-karts, the Niagara Skywheel, and lots of places to eat!

Right beside Rainbow Bridge, which connects Ontario to New York, you can visit Bird Kingdom, the world's largest free-flying indoor aviary.

If you like water parks, then you can spend a night or two at Great Wolf Lodge. Here you can go on all the fun indoor water rides! There's a wave pool, a water treehouse, a lazy river, and many slides!

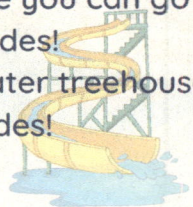

Travel
Journal

My Passport

this is me

Name:_____

Age:_____

my fingerprint

Height:_____

My city:_____ and country:_____

My school: _____

My grade: _____

My best friend(s):_____

My favorite colour(s): _____

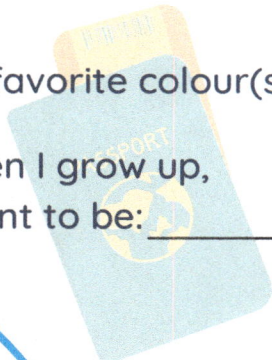

When I grow up,
I want to be:_____

Traveling to:

This is my _____ time going to Toronto.
(1st, 2nd, etc.)

Travel date: _____ _____ , _____
(month)   (day)   (year)

Staying for: _____ days and _____ nights.

Traveling with: _____

Traveling by:

 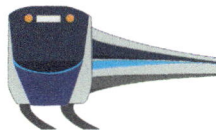

My Packing List

#	Item	✓	#	Item	✓
	T-Shirts			Toothbrush Toothpaste	
	Long-Sleeved Shirts			Books	
	Shorts			Pencil Case	
	Pants			Toys	
	Pajamas				
	Underwear				
	Socks				
	Hats				
	Shoes				

What else might you need? If you are going in the summer, don't forget your swimwear and sunscreen! In the winter, don't forget your coat and winter accessories!

My Travel Plan

The top three places that I want to visit are:

The foods I look forward to trying are:

I'm feeling   about this trip.

excited   nervous

Don't forget to show this page to your grown-ups and plan your Toronto trip together!

Where I'm Staying

I'm staying at:_____

Inside it looks like this:

Outside it looks like this:

I went to _____

on _____ _____, _____.

Weather was:
(circle)

I felt:
(circle)

Draw and write about your visit. What was the best part?

_____
_____
_____

I went to _____
(place)

on _____ _____, _____.
(month)   (day)   (year)

Weather was:
(circle)

I felt:
(circle)

Draw and write about your visit. What was the best part?

I went to _____
(place)

on _____ _____, _____.
(month)   (day)   (year)

Weather was:
(circle)

I felt:
(circle)

Draw and write about your visit. What was the best part?

_____

_____

_____

I went to _____
(place)

on _____ _____, _____.
(month)   (day)   (year)

Weather was:
(circle)

I felt:
(circle)

Draw and write about your visit. What was the best part?

Colour the Beaver

How does a beaver get online?

Answer: By logging on!

I went to _____
(place)

on _____ _____, _____.
(month)   (day)   (year)

Weather was:
(circle)

I felt:
(circle)

Draw and write about your visit. What was the best part?

_____

_____

_____

I went to _____
(place)

on _____ _____, _____.
(month)　　　　(day)　　　(year)

Weather was:
(circle)

I felt:
(circle)

Draw and write about your visit. What was the best part?

I went to _____
(place)

on _____ _____, _____.
(month)   (day)   (year)

Weather was:
(circle)

I felt:
(circle)

Draw and write about your visit. What was the best part?

_____

_____

_____

_____

Sudoku

Fill in the blanks with the missing letters. Make sure the same letter doesn't repeat in a row, a column, or inside the same mini grid.

A   B   C   D   E   F

		F	E		
E		A			
B				F	
	A				B
			F		D
		B	C		

Answers on page 79

I went to _____
(place)

on _____ _____, _____.
(month)   (day)   (year)

Weather was:
(circle)

I felt:
(circle)

Draw and write about your visit. What was the best part?

_____

_____

_____

_____

I went to _____
(place)

on _____ _____, _____.
(month)   (day)   (year)

Weather was:
(circle)

I felt:
(circle)

Draw and write about your visit. What was the best part?

I went to _____
(place)

on _____ _____, _____.
(month)   (day)   (year)

Weather was:
(circle)

I felt:
(circle)

Draw and write about your visit. What was the best part?

I went to _____
(place)

on _____ _____ , _____ .
(month)   (day)   (year)

Weather was:
(circle)

I felt:
(circle)

Draw and write about your visit. What was the best part?

I went to _____
(place)

on _____ _____ , _____ .
(month)   (day)   (year)

Weather was:
(circle)

I felt:
(circle)

Draw and write about your visit. What was the best part?

Toronto Word Hunt

While you are out, see what things you can spot that start with the letters in
T-O-R-O-N-T-O.

T
O
R
O
N
T
O

I went to _____
(place)

on _____ _____, _____.
(month)   (day)   (year)

Weather was:
(circle)

I felt:
(circle)

Draw and write about your visit. What was the best part?

I went to _____
(place)

on _____ _____, _____.
(month)   (day)   (year)

Weather was:
(circle)

I felt:
(circle)

Draw and write about your visit. What was the best part?

_____

_____

_____

I went to _____

on _____ _____, _____.

Weather was:

I felt:

Draw and write about your visit. What was the best part?

I went to _____
(place)

on _____ _____, _____.
(month)   (day)   (year)

Weather was:
(circle)

I felt:
(circle)

Draw and write about your visit. What was the best part?

_____

_____

_____

Trip Highlights

The best part of the trip was...

The coolest thing I did was...

The weirdest thing I saw was....

The yummiest thing I ate was...

The thing that surprised me
the most was...

Next time I visit Toronto,
I want to...

Doodle Pages

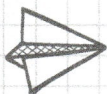

Toronto

Toronto

Toronto

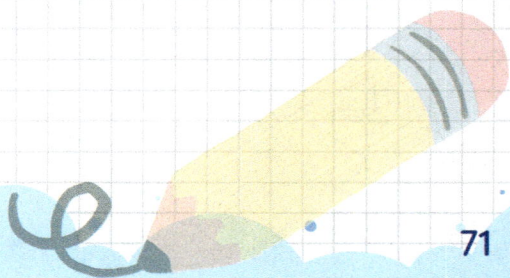

Toronto

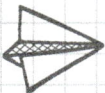

Toronto

Toronto

Toronto

Souvenirs

Use these pages to glue, tape, or staple: tickets, wristbands, pictures, or other items you would like to keep from your adventures exploring the city.

Fun Day!

Answer Key

Page 7 - Toronto Word Search.

```
D P A R K S R G E I N O O T X
Y T I S R E V I D C E O U H V
S K Y S C R A P E R S R R I F
A I K D M E R U T N E V D A O
M U I I C E S O A T G T N H I
A V Y I I N R E Y G O O J E R
P Z D N Y O B W F R H U Y T A
L M O M N M U S E U M S D I T
E O A T E W O F G V B U N N N
L D O A T T R A C T I O N S O
E U E U K P D V P A D A N A C
A I J R P N I P Y T I C L J E
F E R O L P X E A I E N P U U
```

Page 11 - Count the Snacks.

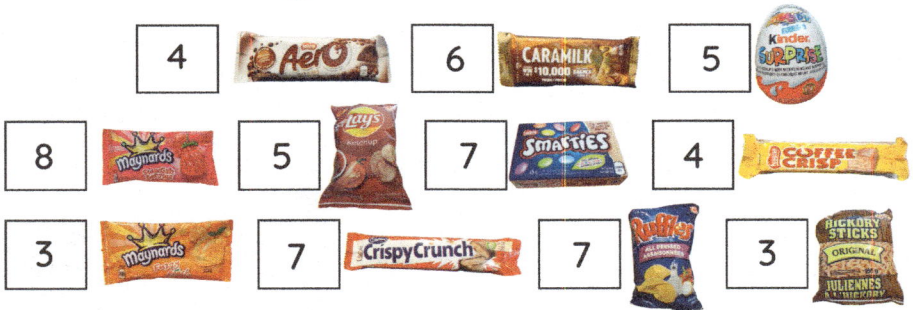

4	Aero	6	CARAMILK	5	Kinder SURPRISE
8	Maynards	5	Lays	7	SMARTIES	4	COFFEE CRISP
3	Maynards	7	Crispy Crunch	7	Ruffles	3	HICKORY STICKS

Page 25 - Match the Toronto Sports Teams.

1 - e, 2 - b, 3 - a, 4 - c, 5 - d

Page 27 - Colour the Toronto Flag.

Answer Key

Page 31 - Name that Food.
a - churro, b - dim sum, c - takoyaki,
d - bungeoppang, e - gulab jamun,
f - phở, g - soufflé pancake, h - taco,
i - beignet

Page 33 - Name that Dinosaur.
1 - Brachiosaurus, 2 - Velociraptor, 3 - Triceratops,
4 - Stegosaurus, 5 - Ankylosaurus,
6 - Tyrannosaurus Rex (T-Rex)

Page 35 - American Sign Language.
Message: TIME TO EXPLORE

Page 57 - Sudoku.

C	B	F	E	D	A
E	D	A	B	C	F
B	E	D	A	F	C
F	A	C	D	E	B
A	C	E	F	B	D
D	F	B	C	A	E

73543180R00044